River and Hills: voices of Irwell

also contains
Poem Seeds

Aziz Dixon

Copyright © 2015 Aziz Dixon
All rights reserved.
ISBN: 1517211913
ISBN-13: 978 1517211912

CreateSpace Independent Publishing Platform,
North Charleston, SC 29406
USA.

ACKNOWLEDGEMENTS

I would like to thank:

Philip Tansen O'Donohoe, my guide and friend,
and my beloved wife Anne for sharing the journey with me.

....

Other titles by Aziz Dixon include:
- Sufi Sunrise
- North Wales Pilgrim: a poetic journey

CONTENTS: RIVER AND HILLS

1	Hiraeth	5
2	It's grim up North	6
3	May the gods protect this town	8
4	Building a nest	10
5	Look what I made today	11
6	Living simply	12
7	Irwell Vale – finding a mate	13
8	Leading with words	14
9	Once in a blue moon	15
10	My midnight garden	16
11	Feed the birds	17
12	Preston and Kathmandu	18
13	Make friends with dervishes	19
14	Windows on life	20

Hiraeth

'Have ever you seen the like of this?'
the care-taker said to me.
'I love this chapel, I love these hills,
this green, always-green,
the saints and the spirits of home.
Hiraeth we call it,'
the pull of the place where I belong.

I know this well, as we pass Peel Tower,
or crest the top of the Grane,
and there in the Valley is Rawtenstall,
a ribbon-flower enfolded by moors,
a garden of peace and plenty.

Hiraeth – is it Ishkh as well,
the longing of Love,
Lover and Beloved in One,
the place inside
where I belong?

It's grim up North

'It's grim up North,' the southern Jessies say,
but really it's a bit of a blur
north of Watford. The Inuit of course
have fifty words for snow, but up North
you hardly notice the rain.

There's stair-rod rain (for cats and dogs),
horizontal too (as on the day we bought our house),
ordinary everyday rain (our national pride),
and the soft cloud which half hides Peel Tower
and gently clings to the top of the moor –
all leaving its blessing before
blowing on over-hill to the land
where the white roses grow.

Not for me the endless urban sprawl
overlaid on the lavender fields of Surrey.
Not for me the planners' utopia ten miles square,
each block of mile-wide concrete sameness
a dark Satanic monotony
same-smothering the earth, the history.

Here, history lives in the mills and hills –
no manicured lawns nor entrance fee:
the curlew keeps this site, and
we can explore, discover
the incline the quarry-men toiled to build,
the broken remains of the polishing mill,
smoothing stones for London feet to walk upon.

I love this Valley of Stone,
Clough-folded in the slope of the hill.
I will lift up mine eyes to the hills,
from whence cometh my help
and my inspiration. Transplanted,
here I belong, here blossom.
It's grim up north, they say,

but who'd ha' thowt it?

May the gods protect this town

Growth and Progress built this town,
the mills – mostly gone (the railway too),
the contour-hugging back-to-backs,
fine chapels, and other monuments
to civic pride; our garden sits on a heap
of slag from the gas-works, greener now
than Eden might have been.

Growth and Progress came back fifty years ago
snaking southerners' lines on the map,
wormed deep holes in the fabric of town –
a church, a graveyard, whole villages too;
but they granted us then
a concrete retail temple,
now demolished at last.

Now the gods have come calling again.
Again they want sacrifice.
At Asda the planner-priests sit, in consultation:
please tell them what you think.
At Asda-on-Limey you can see the moors
for miles around, from Holly Mount,
at Asda, glaring white, where the mill
used to be. At Tesco-on-Irwell
you can see the heron,
the dipper, and sometimes a mink.
At Lidl-on-Irwell still you can see
the old town hall.

But the planners said,
'It's already dead,
that derelict old town hall;
our glass and steel
will surely appeal, and
investment will follow for sure.'
(Go to the foot of our stairs –
Prosperity Cottages, Progressive Cottages

are writ in stone at the terrace-ends
 in the very next street.)

This time the gods demand
the old town hall, seeing not
'the skill of the stonemason,
the carefully crafted design'
at one with the Valley of Stone.
They decree a bus station: 'It shall be
the life and the soul of this place,'
they say.

Are not the gods insatiable?
Who will visit by bus
when everything special has gone?

O Growth, O Progress, please hear me now – help us
connect the past with the future
in this special place!

To the older gods I turn, feeling
the cobbles wet beneath my feet,
where the River rages too, brown-torrenting
after last night's rain.
'Life is a bridge – keep moving to grow;
don't get stuck with your rage.
Allaha abaru,'
I hear. I look up
to the Hills, the god
who forgives and reclothes
the scars of a hundred years ago.
Hills speak as well –
many are the voices flowing in me,
iconoclast and priest, planner and visionary,
the money-counter, the dispossessed
and the traveller, the pilgrim:
all want to speak for the polis.
May they all be heard,
for the health of my being.
All are part of River and Hills.

Building a nest

Precarious now, this office life,
more so than other roosts I have had,
like the nest in the tree
outside my window.

Over the weeks the magpies have
piled it thick, stick upon stick
in squalls of snow, sun shafting through clouds.

Over the months I have clutched at straws –
how, really, does it work here?
Who is to blame today?
… smiles curdled by power.

Now back to my nest, maybe to rest,
no more the bus before dawn.
Spring this time is just for us.

Here too the magpies are building,
high on the hill,
eating chips off the street,
fetching twigs from 'our' land.

Not ours, but guardians we,
for frogs, fox and badger, raven and geese,
neighbours all for the magpies.

Time now to treasure bright gems,
each other, this place,
this spring unfolding.
When do magpies retire?

Look what I made today

I am five, and I go to school now.
Look what I made today!
All 42 of us made some marmalade –
my favourite, oh, and Mrs Etherington,
she helped us too, you know.

I am fifteen, and I don't make things,
so there isn't much to say.
In my class we study hard
in case we make it
to Oxbridge one day.
Nothing else matters.

I am 59, and I don't go out to work
any more. Today
I made a compost bin
from bits of shed and a brick or two.
I designed it all myself. Yes!
It feels like I'm five again,
the fizzing, buzzing 'yes I can'
(I always could but I must have lost it
along the way).

And now as well
I can play with words,
when they feel,
when they tell me what it is
they need to say.

Living simply

The phone rang as I was chopping wood.
A serious business, this -
without an excess of wood we could be, would be
cold or poor, or both
in the winter of our lives.
Now we live simply, we grow our own veg
in the kitchen garden at Frog Palace.
Simply wonder-ful it is.

The voice on the phone explained –
'Full-time-permanent, just-your-skills, give it some thought,'
and my heart replied to my head,
'100 miles and twelve hours a day, or more,
corporate politics too. Is it not OK
to live simply?'

Back in my log-pile I met
the frog: simply living he was, eating
an insect (I think). Brown
more than green, with spots of black, maybe
he bred this year in our pond (his pond?).
(Young frogs are everywhere these days.)
Without a log-pile
he might be cold or poor, or both,
next winter.

He looked me in the eye, warily, and
I breathed him peace,
hopping on the breath,
hoping he will, simply, be well.

Irwell Vale – finding a mate

Lightly we walk by the river;
ruin and rubble are greening now,
for spring is a hundred shades of fresh green,
a kingfisher-flash of the rainbow
darts downstream. Dipper dips,
its colours dark and light,
like the play of the water in millstones,
the babble and splash, chunnering cheerfully.

Beyond the bridge, two shy souls,
walking out, splashing out together,
looking for a private place
to call their own, the ideal home
for goosanders,
the right sort of bank for nesting.

When did they meet?
Were they both from round here?
This tender attraction needs no words –
spring blesses us both,
my mate and me.

Leading with words

When he was a lad
he had something to prove,
only just in his teens,
new kid on the block.
British bulldog, he led them to win,
life and death it was
to him.

Thus he instructed, when
muddling at work, we had
the leadership blues.
'Find the spark,' he said,
'Lead from within.
That's what I did
at Goose Green – not boy scout, but
o/c for real. I led from the front.'

Now 30 years on, TV replay,
Falklands, shot by shot,
death by death, just as it was then.
For what did they die,
in that desolate place?

Today *we* had war,
on our border it was.
With his chain-saw, the uncle
cut to pieces her trees.
Police and invective, dead limbs,
shattered dreams. This
desecration where she played
years ago as a child.
Old man next door, had you
something still to prove?

Life is a battle,
if we word it thus,
but why need it be
so much them-and-us?

Once in a blue moon

Your lock of hair I found
on the path, a curl of white,
when I went out early to see
what the new day brings.
I, curious to know who had come
visiting the sanctuary while
we were not there.

Last night we watched the blue moon
rise, full and clear and bright above the hills,
and we left the bats on night-shift
(the owls maybe are on holiday,
for I've not heard them calling of late;)
and we went in to compline,
our appreciation moment
which rounds off the day.

Now with first light of dawn I open the gate,
cross the threshold to our other world.
I sniff the air, smell the wet earth,
eager to find what has changed overnight.
More berries, more crops, but the corn
struggles still. The pond's fuller now –
please tell the frogs. The peace
still the same as by moonlight it was.

How old you are I cannot tell
from your hair – maybe not so young.
Last night you came without waking
the dogs. Your routes underground
I sense – I found one once when planting a tree.
I wish I could meet you, badger,
once in a blue moon.

My midnight garden

Quick – where's Miss Marple?
The killer has struck once again.
I was indoors at the time,
watching her solve a crime
(so I have an alibi.)

When I bid goodnight to the garden
all was sweetness (tomatoes ripening)
and light (from the stars);
no creepy music, no flitting shadows,
no clues such as
sinister oozing slime; and
I guess the marauding pigeons
were safely at rest in their roosts.

But now, even before breakfast
there are corpses everywhere,
the best of the crop.
How they fought back is
a mystery to me (please ask the sleuth),
but the cabbages, tender young things,
have killed every slug in sight.

Feed the birds

Feed the birds – two pounds a bag
(a small bag, from the bargain shop). Perhaps
Mary Poppins can help with this one:
who was it abducted the bird feeder,
and ate all the seeds as well?

Our privy does multi-tasking –
'bird hide' is not just a euphemism.
Here we can sit, quietly, and watch…
the robin, the dunnock, sometimes a flock
of long-tailed tits and their cousins
(no stale peanuts please – we only want them fresh!)
Sometimes Hitchcock inspires the jackdaws,
too many to count, feeding in frenzy.
Even the pigeon, intellectually challenged,
can fit under the roof
on the bird table now.

But twice in a week the feeder has
gone for a walk. (First time,
it did not come back.) Might it be
the Big Cat of Rossendale, or
the heron, whose prints we think we found,
stalking warily up from the pond?

No, today the suspect is
an earth bear (as they say in Wales),
maybe a slim teenager rampaging
at night – the hedgehog gap in the fence
is too small to admit a bird feeder,
but snout-scuffles in the lawn, and
a scat-clue or two suggest it was
young Tommy Brock. I'd better keep vigil
all night – or maybe I'll just
have a word with his mother.

Preston and Kathmandu
April 2015

Who happily blessed this straight suburban street
with cherry trees, as far as the I can see?
So many thousand blossoms,
each flower becoming perfection,
leading the eye from tree to tree
along the road we take.

Now dead in a truck, the branches lie.
Traffic swirls and snarls on the motorway.
A 'surgeon for trees' – but who
could surgically cut such a tree
when in blossom?

So many thousand souls,
each one becoming perfection,
live far away in a place so wrecked.
Not statistics but each with a name,
a mother, a face, an I.

Send surgeons! Send planes with supplies!
The earthquake demands no less.
All dead in the crush, the crash
of concrete and dust.
Who can bless them now
with blossoms so fragile
and pink?

Make friends with dervishes

Far away, green Sufism is spreading fast,
showing us, if we needed reminding,
how we should care for our earth, this world.

No fracking here, the car-sign pleads; but
what is mine to do?
Here is such an abundance:
the hedgerow offers apples and pears, plums,
berries, and cherries enough
for the squirrel as well. In the fields
cornflowers vie with potatoes for space.
Above the age-old oaks, and taller still,
the dervishes turn, turbine arms rotating
slowly, in unison.

At home on the moors, where they'd frack us too
the dervishes stand, and they spoil the view;
our life is abundant and green,
but maybe we need them now more than ever.
Is it now time to make friends
with our own wind-whirling dervishes?

Windows on life

Now we see through a glass, darkly
For my freshly-cut aching grief
for my dear departed sister
my professor counsels Boethius,
The Consolation of Philosophy.
She distracts me with Bede,
her personal friend of many years.
Having dug where he lived,
uncovered floors he may have walked on,
she knows just where 'his' window-glass
was found, where it belonged
on the monastic site we explore
at Jarrow.

but then, face to face;
Face to face with Bach, dissolving
in the One, I see through the window as we sing.
This frame, holding the pine tree,
the Alpine slopes, etched on my memory,
it sustains me still, keeps fresh for me
my first sufi awakening,
at Campra in Ticino.

now I know in part;
Through my office window I watch
as they disfigure a cedar of Lebanon
after two hundred years: diseased, they say,
but they leave it
with stumps for limbs, a *blessé de guerre*.
Soon, I foresee, the organisation
will go the same way, and only in part
can I make sense of my life just now,
in Milton Keynes.

but then shall I know, even as I am known.
This window on the garden we tend with such love
frames the rose, the freshly-cut flower
we planted on our first anniversary.
It flourishes now, two years later.
Like the Trimurti,
like the knower, the known and the knowing,
you and I, the rose and the perceiving,
love, lover and beloved, we
merge in the heart of the One,
inside, and here at home, on Irwell.

Poem Seeds

Aziz Dixon

CONTENTS: POEM SEEDS

1	Magnificat, in D	24
2	How did he know?	25
3	Paper trail	26
4	You'll be a Man, my son	28
5	Flowers for Charlie	29
6	Finding water	30
7	Easter in Leeds	31
8	Little wizard	32
9	Per ardua ad astra	33
10	Where can I buy a froe?	34
11	Close at heart	35
12	Early one morning	36

Magnificat, in D

The morning sun is already hot
on my back as I kneel to pick
the fruit the birds have left.
Each ripe redcurrant, eucharistic red,
filtering sunlight like an angel in glass;
each berry with its seed of potential,
something so small with a message so
particular.
Just so, each poem starts as seed;
some fall by the wayside, some
bear fruit more than others.

And music does not grow on trees,
but perhaps that too comes from seeds.
What shape, what texture are music seeds?
As when Bach wrote, quoting Mary's song of fullness,
Magnificat anima mea,
my soul doth magnify the Lord,
and my spirit hath rejoiced in God my Saviour.

How did he know?
Cadair Idris, 1964

He has been this way before me,
training squaddies, this leader of men,
his life mapped out.

I but a boy, in awe at the bluebells,
this rock - big as a cottage,
this rain - 'It rains a lot in Wales, you know,'
says Dad.

We climb, the sea lost in fog.
We walk, we drip, the sheep don't mind.
Now to eat lunch. Rain
drips in my boots.

'Above and beyond is the summit,
over there is the lake.'
Wind wipes clouds, gently lifts the sky.
Sun glints on the water,
the lake a jewel below us.
How did he know it was
there?

Paper trail

In the mirror I glimpse
your face, his face. Your short legs
I know I have, like father, like son,
but may I not inherit dementia,
your father's or yours; and your love of filing
has quite passed me by.
I think
you no longer know who I am, but
this morning we touched, you accepted
a drink and some music.

Now, in your office, I fetch the papers
you marked out for shredding
from the serried ranks of your files
which line all these walls.
Is this how your mind is now?
A letter of pain held for twenty years
next to stationery bills just as old,
customer service indignation,
replies to God
as channelled by your sister,
records of health, wealth and wine
all now scattered and jumbled.
Here, where you used to compose,
transcribe, create, to arrange,
to order and control.

Filing is not my forte,
I don't clean my shoes, army-style, every day,
but there's so much to inherit –
your love of mountains,
your access to music divine,
the 'I can' of your carpentry,
your patterns of striving, providing,
each of them footprints in my life.

Wherever your mind is now
I cannot guess, but
may your heart be at rest,
may you inherit peace
from your son.

You'll be a Man, my son

Swallows and Amazons, hobbits and dragons,
even Nero the goat (a family creation) –
all seemed more real when shared
with my daughters three
at the end of the day; but
for Kipling I had no son.

'If you will come with me…'
my father said one day…
and so it was we left our home
on chalk and flint in the lee
of a hillfort (a 'place of wealth and power'
three thousand years ago).

We travelled into the dusk
along the track the ancestors took,
over downs and through the woods,
(past rabbits scattered dead
on an industrial scale); finding
in time the suitable place,
we brewed a rabbit-free meal,
shielded from the dying wind
in a hillfort ditch ramparting
the highest point. We talked,
as the stars replaced the setting sun,
a spark for the man I could become.

Seeking my roots in the land,
in my ancestors and the wild outdoors,
learning to love and be loved,
to be gentle and strong
as befits my birth-name,
to bequeath more joy from the One
than the sorrows I have lived –
if these I can achieve, then maybe
I too will be a Man.

Flowers for Charlie
Durham

Celandines by first light in spring,
wild in the wood they grow,
just as they did that day
all those years ago,
when you chose
to go.

One pressed on a card you sent me,
the last that I heard from you.

Yet what do I know
that they could not say?
What was it like each day
to nurse you, to comfort you,
sister, daughter, and friend?

By the river we laid you,
but I could not find you there.
Less often now, but still
in my dreams you come to me,
as hale as you used to be.

In the music you played
I hear you again.
Your art in our home
bursts off the walls,
inspiring, connecting.
Stay well til we meet once again.

Celandines flowering still,
wild in that wood they grow.

Finding water
Ashton, 1976

A scorching brown drought
bakes the once-green fields of middle England.
Harvest is dry as the dust in our hair,
the dust to which we return.

Layer by layer we dissect
the warm earth, reading life
into changes of colour, patterns of stones.

Deeper we dig, deeper still -
shoring and safety need practical skills.
A well on the site, how deep can we go?
The mill-stream nearby but a sun-dappled trickle.

Who dug here for water, did they think
they were 'Romans,' and what were their names?
Now plumbing the depths, we winch from the past.
Lead container but yet not a bath;
redeeming clues, a font on this site,
giving water for blessing.

How did it end – why a font down a well?
Next year we will dig here again,
searching for patterns, for voices, connections.

Now homeward bound, I pause
in the porch. This minster,
stone cool in the heat,
this church yet undreamt
when they worshipped Him here.

'Thank you,' I say,
for this life, for their lives,
for stories untold.
As if in reply,
it is *raining* - again!

Easter in Leeds
Good Friday, 2015

Haydn at his most mellifluous,
the programme says.
Cool in the Minster I sit.
The baton raised,
the pause between the in-breath
and
the out-breath, where the worlds meet.

Yes, *I* have sung this as well,
in another time, another place,
rehearsals sandwiched between meetings,
tensions at work dissolved.
Ten years ago, this music lifted my soul.

Now seated, I dance in the aisles,
your hand in mine:
et vitam venturi saeculi, Amen.
Is this the life of the world to come,
with you in my soul?

Who can catch a fugue in words?
Who knows where your breath touches mine?...
this harmony we weave,
the bliss
        sublime.

Little wizard
Llyn Brenig, 26.08.15

At last the tree-skimming gorse-clipping pilots
have roared off to play somewhere else;
the rain, though insistent is distant,
and all I can hear are the waves slap-lapping to shore
once again. On the rolling sweep of the moors
the August purple of heather vies
with the thistle and rose bay willow herb,
and the whinberries taste all purple
and sweet.

Our trail guide is for children,
each Bronze Age wonder
carefully explained, with games and activities,
and a score-list for the wildlife.
No marks out of ten for translation, but we can learn
the English for clochdar y cerrig,
the Welsh for wheatear (male and female),
and many more, the ravens, and,
not ten feet away on a post, a buzzard.

But just as we leave someone flits
from a dead tree to the edge of the wood;
she (as I think) starts preening herself
as if for the grainy photos we took,
while dodging the traffic. Unseasonal cuckoo?
What is this hawk-owl mystery bird?
She's not on the list, may speak only Welsh,
but when we get home we are sure
we've been face to face with
a merlin.

Per ardua ad astra
Llyn Brenig, 26.08.15

Flight swifter by far than a peregrine,
they Really Are Fast, these birds,
with a very loud startling cry.
They prefer large areas of outstanding natural beauty
and the utmost tranquility;
often to be seen hunting low
over the ground, like a sparrowhawk.

Known to have colonised a Valley
on Anglesey; vagrants occur to the east,
in deserts, where fighting is found,
occasionally elsewhere. May interbreed
(sometimes without proper approval)
with North American subspecies.

Feeds on misunderstanding,
duality and fear. For protection
invoke Allah o Akhbar,
In Peace is Power.

Where can I buy a froe?

They all speak e-speak –
how about you?
I can speak e-speak
when I have to.
I prefer my Apples crunchy, though
it's not PC to say so, and I can't
virtually find an e-froe anywhere.
It's the latest must-have gismo,
so I'm told.

I've looked in an e-bay,
on the Amazon river of commerce:
there might be one from Muller
in Austria, hand-forged, traditional,
with fine beech handles, and
a mallet to match.
No good for kindle-ing, but fine
for the firewood, better at
splitting logs than infinitives.

Don't froe the (face)book at me –
it'll give me a splitting headache.
I don't need a tablet, or an eye-pad,
I haven't got a happy-app,

I just want to chop wood.

Close at heart

Close at heart, though miles apart,
in the dark I curl my toes,
gripping the wet mossy lawn, as
we speak by phone. I love
the way you speak.
Before sleep I appreciate you
as I always do each day –
hard to find fresh words each night
to explain my gratitude, but each night
there is more to say.

Now with the glimmer of dawn
I toss and turn, I ache
to feel you next to me,
skin soft against skin, every pore
loving you. Heart to heart I send
my love on the breath, making light
of the miles apart. Rumi
has so much to say –
it's like you were always
inside me. Soon
we may be kissing,

but not soon enough,
my Beloved.

Early one morning

Early one so-still morning
I walked alone in a southern wood,
many a motorway mile from home;
alone, but reading as you might
the holy book of Nature, the outward signs
of sacred stillness: the shape
of a dappled leaf, the pearls of dew
on a blackberry ripening,
the squirrel at breakfast, tail curled with focus,
and the woodpecker's yaffle and tap.

Then it was I found the garden,
memorial to a poet beyond duality now,
with heath and vetch, and fungi
two hands tall, and in the pond
lilies which you'd love,
waiting to open in the sun.

And so it was I called to mind
our garden, our love, the seeds
we plant. What we nurture flourishes here,
within. May this
be our memorial.
Ya Ghani.

Notes

Hiraeth was first published in my collection: North Wales Pilgrim: a poetic journey.

Make friends with Dervishes was first published in my collection: Sufi Sunrise.

Made in the USA
Charleston, SC
18 November 2015